Etsy for Beginners

The Ultimate Guide to Making Killer Profits
Selling on Etsy

Copyright © 2015

Table of Contents

Introduction

I want to thank you and congratulate you for downloading the book, "Etsy for Beginners: *The ultimate guides to making a killer profit selling on Etsy*".

This book contains proven steps and strategies for you to build a successful Etsy store and to make profits from selling your crafts on the Etsy website.

If you have a passion for handcrafting things and have always dreamt of sharing your talent with the rest of the world, then Etsy is the perfect place for you to market your products for the whole world to see. The beautiful little things that you have till now made just for family and friends, that everybody loved – you can now sell them to potential customers and make a living for yourself!

Still many questions arise: Is it possible to make a living selling on Etsy? Is it possible to make profit? Can I do it?

This book is the ultimate guide to all those questions and more. Here, you will learn everything there is to know about Etsy, what you can and cannot sell, and how you can generate sales and profit by selling your product.

Thanks again for downloading this book, I hope you enjoy it!

Chapter 1: Know all about Etsy

Are your really good at making something? Like the beaded jewelry for Mardi gras that everyone says are better than the ones you can buy in the store? Are the quilts you made for your baby the envy of all mothers in your neighborhood? Did you have a hobby of making adorable little wooden furniture before you left it for a high-paying job that you don't even like?

What if there was a way for you to make money - not just a pittance, but enough to make it into an important second income selling them?

Not just that? Is your house full of vintage furniture and tidbits that you inherited from your great-grandmother that you will probably not be using? Like an ancient box of fancy buttons your aunt left you when you don't even like to sew? A grand piano, dating back to the 60s, that you have no space in your house for? Some vintage jewelry that are pretty expensive and that you love, but they are not really 'you'?
Now you have a place to sell them, at a good price, to actual people who will appreciate them!

And finally, do you have access to quality supplies and tools like wood, cotton, paper and fabrics? Even beads, buttons and the like? Things that will help other people create handmade things at home, either for themselves or for the purpose of selling? Are you having trouble finding people who are in need of these quality supplies, and in a small amount? Then, you have somewhere to sell them!

If you are someone who can relate to any or more of the three categories mentioned above, if you have something to sell, a gift to share with people who will appreciate your talent and handiwork, if you want to make your hobby into a sustainable income - Etsy is the perfect platform for you!

But first, let's know a few things about Etsy and how it can help you grow.

What is Etsy?

If we give you a professional definition, Etsy is an e-commerce website, a platform where thousands of online sellers and buyers gather to trade hand-crafted good, vintage items and crafting supplies. Literary thousands of artist, crafters and designers are selling their crafts and sharing their talent with buyers who appreciate a touch of something unique and different in their lives other than something common that is found in malls and supermarkets.

The items that you can sell on Etsy cover a wide range: from handcrafted toys to vintage jewelry, baked goods to old furniture, craft supplies to paintings, pottery to photographs.

That brings us to a question of what you can sell on Etsy.

What can you sell on Etsy?

Everything that you can sell on Etsy can be divided into three categories:

- **Everything Handmade**

Almost everything that you can craft with your hands that you think will seem appealing to other people, you can sell on Etsy. This includes all kinds of things ranging from a batch of homemade cookies to a wooden crib for babies.

Are you really good at painting, and can finish around 6/7 paintings in a year? Why not try to sell them on Etsy so that you can share your gift with the world and earn a little money on the side?

Have you always worn T-shirts that you prefer to screen-print yourself? Now, spread your hobby around, and sell them to others who would like to buy your T-shirts.

Did you always prefer making sock puppets for your children, because you liked how they enjoyed a toy that you made for them? Perhaps other people would also like to buy one of your creations for their children!

What are the other things that you can do?

Perhaps you have a habit of up-cycling, i.e. taking something old and making it into something usable. Such as cutting up an old jeans and making it into a sling back, or a pair of coasters. Or, using an old oversized T-shirt to make into a handy apron. You can sell both types on Etsy.

Do you have someone helping you making these crafts, i.e. are more than your two hands crafting them? Someone like a spouse, a child or a sibling? Or even the girl next door that you have hired to help you for the summer? Maybe an assistant who will supervise the work while you are away at your chores or your main job? Either ways, you can sell your products on Etsy.

- **Vintage Items**

If you have a house full of vintage items and antiques that you have no place to store and no wish to use, you can always sell them on Etsy to people who are fond of the same things.

But what qualifies as vintage item? Anything that is more than 20 years old and is rightfully yours can be sold.

Did a great-aunt have a habit of collecting designer bags into the early 70s that is now in your possession? Sell them on Etsy to other people who collect the same thing now.

Still have your grandmother's marriage bed but it doesn't fit in your modern interiors? Sell it to a person who loves vintage furniture.

Did you inherit your family's library but you are more of an eBook and gadget kind of person? Some people love to collect old books and first editions. They would love to get them out of your hands!

The only limitation is that these things have to be older than 20 years to be sold on Etsy.

- **Supplies**

Since Etsy is a platform that is mainly focused in promoting the crafting community, any supplies that other people can use for making and handcrafting their products is also allowed to be sold on Etsy.

So, if you have a supply of beads or designer buttons, if you can provide wood for amateur carpenters or wool for people who knit, you can sell these items on Etsy. Also, if you specialize in design that people can sew, or strips of clothes for others to make into quilts, you can also go on to Etsy to sell them to people who are looking for the exact same thing.

Do you make your own paint to tie-dye your clothes, or your own paper? You can sell them to other people who also practice tie dye or are looking for recycled paper to make into cards and notebooks.

That, in a nutshell, are all the things that you are allowed to sell on Etsy. However, before you are ready to gather up your merchandise, you will also have to know of the items that you can't sell here.

What can you *not* sell on Etsy?

The things that you can and cannot sell on Etsy are almost inter related, so you need to be clear on your merchandise to see if they are eligible.

- You cannot sell something that you have assembled and not crafted, something that came in a 'Do-it-yourself' package, such as a 'Paint-by-numbers' painting, or a guided sewing set that came with a design, tools and materials.
- You cannot re-sell anything that you have haven't crafted yourself. Etsy is not a platform for buying and selling second-hand goods. So, unless the tea-set that you are trying to sell has been hand crafted by you and not a gift from your mother in law, you cannot sell it on Etsy.

- You cannot sell your services on Etsy; it would have to be a physical and concrete object. You can't advertise yourself as a baby-sitter, a house-cleaner, a dog-walker or a masseur on Etsy. (However, you can advertise your talents as a designer or a writer, and sell people your books and your designs.)
- You cannot sell any commercialized item that you have only repackaged and redecorated. For example, you cannot sell a gift basket that is packed with products that you bought at the store. If your gift basket is filled with hand-sewn clothes, or homemade muffins, then it can be sold on Etsy.
- You cannot sell anything that is illegal, such as drugs and drug like substances, firearms, hazardous and flammable substances, pornography or smoking materials. You can also not sell live animals or human body parts (except hair and teeth) on Etsy.

So, if you are trying to turn your hobby or a talent into your income source, there are a lot of things that you can choose from to sell at Etsy. All you have to find out is where our talent lies.

Chapter 2: How to Sell your Talent on Etsy

Welcome to the world of Etsy, where your talents are marketable and will bring you a cool check at the end of every month.

Up till now, you may have just made scrapbooks for your friends and cute little outfits for your children. But with Etsy, you will really be able to just get online and sell those things to other people and get paid in the process. If up until now, you have been getting paid in smiles, 'thank you's and gratitude, now is the time to actually make some money!

In this chapter we will show you a few steps on how to get ready for a career (part-time or full-time) on Etsy!

Find out what you want to do

Of course, the first thing that you really need is a hobby, a preference - something that you like to do and something that you are good at doing.

As you see, there are two aspects to this: something that you like, as well as something that you are good at. It has to be something that you like because most people who sell their crafts on Etsy do it because that thing was their hobby or a pastime at past. If you are making something that you are not fond of, or that you don't like, it actually ridicules the whole idea. Can you build a career out of selling your paintings if you don't like to paint? Can you make vintage clothes if you don't like sewing, or clothes, or designs?

So, first of all, find something that you like to do, and then act on it.

Second is, this is something that you have to be good at, so good that people who don't know you would want to buy it for money and use it themselves. It's no use if you love to do something but is not that good at it; your parents and your family would appreciate it, but not strangers who will want to spend money for it.

Have you found something that you love to do, and is good it? Great!

Expand the Idea behind it

For the purpose of an example, let's say that it is sewing that you are passionate about. Nothing is more enjoyable to you than some clothes, scissors, needles and threads, and time on your hand. You have always worn clothes that you have made; your children love the colorful costumes that you make for them. You have also always made quilts and baby clothes as gifts for all your friends and relatives.

Let's expand on the idea.

There's a lot that you can do with that skill. Out of everything that you can do with clothes and sewing tools, which one do you want to work on?

Perhaps the one thing that you want to do is make baby clothes - comfortable and inexpensive clothes for new born babies that are gorgeous but at the same time, will cost much less than clothes that are sold by designer brands and at the malls. I'm sure the new mothers would really appreciate it.

So, you have decided on your craft - clothes for newborn babies! Let's proceed to the next step.

Put in some research

No one should ever go into something without the adequate amount of research needed. After you have decided on a craft, you need to do a lot of market research into your product before you actually start to sell them.

Your market research will have to include:

- **Similar ideas/products on Etsy:** Unless you have come up with something that is literally out of this world, chances are that there are already thousands of others who are selling similar ideas/products on Etsy. While their products and your ideas would not be 100% similar, they will definitely fit the same categories and hold almost the same appeal to your customers. However, friendly competition is nothing to be discouraged of. You are there to sell your products just as they are, and you are going to learn from them, not be frightened by them

- **How the market for your product is:** Just because a product similar to yours is up on Etsy for sale, it doesn't mean that it is selling very well. Research into the demand for those particular kind of objects, and how they are selling on Etsy. If the product that you have in mind is not doing well as a business on Etsy, it might be a better option to change your craft to something else that has a demand.

- **How these products are priced:** You will also need to take a look at how these products are priced at, and whether you can sell yours at similar prices. If someone is selling a similar product at a very low price - a price that you know wouldn't even cover your cost - then, this is not going to be a profitable business for you.
  Also, if someone else is selling baby clothes at a price that is somewhat relatable to you, but their products are not selling because they are deemed to be expensive by the customers - that require a change in plans, too.
- **How these Products are presented:** How others present similar products is important for your research, too. This will give you an idea of what to do with your crafts, if you decide to execute this plan. See how they have described their crafts, how they have listed, what pictures they have uploaded - the overall presentation of the product. This will help you present your craft to your customers, later.

And now is the time to act on your decision. If you have decided on making baby clothes, whip up a batch of your finest work, and we will start on the next step - creating an Etsy store!

Chapter 3: Set up an Etsy Store

The next step for you is to set up an Etsy store, right out of your home. The procedure is easy and hassle free, and with the guidelines provided in this chapter, won't take much of your time.

Familiarize yourself with the Website

The website is www.etsy.com. Remember it because you will need to visit it quite often from now on!

Before you sign up, you will need to familiarize yourself with the Dos and Don'ts of the Etsy website. These guidelines will provide you with a list of what you can and cannot sell on the website (although, you already know that), how to set up the account, how you can maintain your store and all the other rules and regulations that Etsy asks you to follow.

Set up an Etsy Account

Setting up an Etsy account is an easy process that requires your name, an user name, a password to protect your account and an email address where all your mails and notifications would be forwarded to.

You can also choose to sign up for regular newsletters, if you want to be updated all the news and information.

Set up your Etsy Store

Your Etsy store name is really important, for your branding as well as your future. You would want to call it something that would sound witty and practical, something that sounds fun but also makes a lot of sense and relates to your product. Such as, OnceUponATimeTutus are a very popular Etsy store for children's accessories, RivermillEmbroidary is a store that sells embroidered clothes and RubyLoveDesigns sells beautiful baby books.

A few tips on choosing a name:

- When you have thought of a name, run it by etsy.com to see if a similar name exists. Change it, because you don't want to confuse your customers.
- Choose a name that keeps your store open ended, in case you think of expanding your product. You can't start selling baby quilts if you name your store 'OnlyBabyClothes', can you?
- Don't make the name too simple of too difficult to write. Ideally, it should have some word play into it. The name would also be your user name on the website, so don't make it too difficult.

Create your Etsy Banner

The next important thing that you would need is a 760X100 pixels wide banner that would be the primary introduction to your store. The banner is the first thing that all potential customers would see, just like a signboard on the top of an actual store.

Create your Etsy Avatar

Now is the time to introduce yourself - the owner and the crafter - into the equation. Etsy requires the user to create an Avatar - an online presence which requires a clear and distinct photo of yourself, your location and a short description.

Be sure to sound like yourself on your profile, and tell your potential customers who you are, what your hobbies and interests are, and what can you offer them that are special. Your language should be grabbing and interesting, and should be able to hook your customers so that they feel interested to look through your products before moving on to someone else.

Include personal information so that the customers can feel that they know you and can relate to you.

Be sure to mention if you have multiple accounts on Etsy, or if there are more than you working on your product. This is mentioned in the Etsy guidelines.

Create your product Listing

The final step is to list and upload all the products that you are going to provide your customers. Each listing will require a name, a picture, a description and a price. You can also tag in keywords for your products that will help the customers come to your store.

If you have come this far, you have successfully created an Etsy store for your products and you are good to go! However, just like in the real world, opening a store in Etsy doesn't guarantee you sales from the first day.

There are a few ways that you accelerate your business to make profits on Etsy, and that is what we are going to discuss in the next chapter.

Chapter 4: How to make profit with Etsy

Now we have come to the most crucial, and the most important part of this book - how to make profits with Etsy, or how to earn money through Etsy.

So, how much money can you actually make by selling your products on Etsy? Is it a source of passive or secondary income; is it limited to only make money worth your pocket money; or, is it possible to leave your day job and make your Etsy store your main occupation?

The answer is: there is no definite answer. Actually, this is a trick question. Your future with Etsy is exactly how you want it to be. If you are comfortable with your crafts selling moderately, i.e. a dozen orders in six months, then your Etsy store will be a source of moderate income, helping you to build a nest egg, or plan a yearly vacation.

However, if you are passionate about this and want to turn your hobby into your career, it is also possible. You would just have to labor with your Etsy store just as you would toil with a regular job.

The choice, definitely, is yours. But hey —isn't that the dream? How many people have the chance to actually work on something that they love and watch their career flourish at the same time? What was it that Confucius said?

"Choose a job you love and you will never have to work a day in your life."

So let's just assume that we are making this hobby of ours into our main occupation, and hoping to make it into a multi-billion dollar business venture someday. For the time being, we should focus on generating profit.

There are three things that you need to focus on the most when you are trying to generate a significant amount of profit through your Etsy store and trying to build it into a sustainable business: pricing, branding and marketing.

Let us discuss them one by one.

Pricing

Since you are the one making, marketing and selling the product, you should be the one who gets to decide on a price to. So, before you put a price on your product and list it in your Etsy store, these are the things that you should remember:

1. Price of Competition

We are safe to assume that you are not the only person on Etsy who is selling baby clothes, there are others. Before you put a price tag on your product, complete a market research on your competitors. Are all of their products priced in the range of $8-$12/piece? Then perhaps that should be your price range too.

Do you think that the clothes you can provide are of better quality than their? Then you could probably hike your price to $15/piece. But if you price each of your products at $150 while all your competitors are selling theirs at around $10, you are unlikely to sell anything.

2. Cost of Materials

Since you are selling an actual tangible product, you do have a cost price – the money that you have spent in making that product. Some cost prices are easy to calculate, such as the amount of fabric needed to make a particular piece. Or, if you buy threads by the dozen and need one to finish a piece, how much money to count.

In these cases, always try to be fair by including partial costs of the products that are partially used, such as the thread, a roll of lace or buttons.

3. Labor

Yes, you do have to charge the cost of your labor, even for things that you are making at home, in your spare time, out of sheer love for the project.

Think of it this way, of you were giving the same amount of time at a job, you would have got wage for it. So, why not on Etsy?

Calculate the time that you are taking to make each piece and calculate your hourly wage. Or, you can just assign a certain amount, such as $3 or $4 as your labor cost per piece.

4. Other Fees and Payments

There are some other Etsy and PayPal fees that you will have to consider. Please note that Etsy deducts $0.20 per listing of product and 3.5% of the price when your product makes a sale. You have to consider this amount while deciding on a price.

Besides, whether you choose to receive your money via Paypal or Etsy Direct deposit, both processes deduct some money from your earnings.

- PayPal fees are flat $0.30 per transaction and 2.7% of total money collected through monthly sales

- Etsy Direct Deposit is $0.25 per transaction and 3.0% of total money collected through monthly sales

So, whatever price you consider for your product, be sure to take these numbers into consideration.

5. Shipping Costs

You have the products with you, and you have to send them to your customers; therefore, you are the one who has to bear the shipping costs too. So, don't forget to add a precise shipping cost so that it doesn't eat into your profits.

6. Profits

And finally we arrive at the profit. When you have calculated everything else – the cost, the labor, the fees and the shipping, you would still have to consider making a profit! Otherwise, you are just slaving away for nothing but a minimum wage.

Your profit can be the surplus that you are making, or it can be the investment that you are going to use to make your business grow. This amount can be small at the beginning, and increased more and more when your business starts to gather recognition.

After pricing comes another important part of selling: branding.

Branding

When you have decided on the pricing and finally uploaded your product listing, it is time to start selling it. But before that, you will need the customers to come to your store. Here's how you can do that.

- ### Photographs

Remember, your potential customers can't see your products since this is not an actual store, but they can see your photographs. Since a picture is worth a thousand words, this is you cue to take the best photo of your product possible.

When we say photographs, we don't mean shots taken with a phone or Instagram. The photos have to be extremely good – professional, if possible – and should define your product perfectly. Try using natural light and a neutral background; try showing all angles of the product in multiple shots and best yet – try to show them 'in use'.

- ### Categories

Etsy listing gives you a chance to categorize your product. So, chose the category carefully so that you are not stuck in 'Accessories'/'Adults' when you are supposed to be in 'Clothes'/'Infants'.

- ### Tags

You can add as many as 13 tags with each product listing so do take advantage of that. Use as many words as you can think of while tagging your product; including the color, the fabric, the season and the style of the product.

- **A little something extra**

When your customers order a product, they only expect the product to arrive on their doorstep and nothing else. It's the 'something extra' that you can do that will grab their attention and make them come back to you again and again.

So, what can you do to make this a memorable shopping experience for them? Consider adding a little 'thank you' note with each delivery, a tiny gift of a rattle or a pacifier with each product, a business card, or a discount card for the next order. These small gestures will make the customer feel special and loyal.

Marketing

You still have another important job left to do, and that is – marketing your product properly to attract more customers to your store. And this includes not only customers who are already avid Etsy buyers, but outside, too.

Marketing is a concept that has changed remarkably over the last few years. Today, it is possible to market your product with very low or no cost at all.

- **Social Media Marketing**

Social Media is indeed a miracle worker when it comes to marketing your product for free. Platforms like Facebook, Twitter, Instragram and Pinterest not only helps in bringing your product to your customers but also keeps you updated with what they think of your product or what changes and developments they are looking for.

- **Blogs**

If you consider yourself an expert on your product, let the whole world know it through your blogs. Your followers would appreciate your insight into the matter and be pleased about the fact that you take your passion seriously. Besides, blogs are great ways to drive traffic to your products.

- **Search Engine Optimization (SEO)**

SEO is a relatively new concept that will take your products to top of Google lists when someone searches for similar products. These days, you can pay someone to make your products important in Google search that will bring customers into your store.

- **The Grapevine**

Never underestimate the power of word-of-mouth. Ask friends, family members and co-workers to spread the news of your amazing business to their friends and families. Allow a special discount or a prize when your customers come with a recommendation and your business name will spread out wide and far.

- **Newsletters and mailing lists**

Offer your customers to sign up for your monthly newsletters and you can make sure that they will keep coming back for more. Just make sure you have something to keep them interested with every issue.

Just follow these few simple rules, and your Etsy store is bound to earn you the profits and the career that you have always wanted, all the while you are doing something that you love and that you are passionate about.

Here's to a successful career on Etsy!

Conclusion

Thank you again for downloading this book!

I hope this book was able to help you to see ways of how you can start a successful Etsy store and make killer profits on it. If you are interested in starting a career with Etsy, then this is the perfect book for you to read.

The next step is to open a store on Etsy, fill it up with your crafts and make a livelihood selling the things you love to the people who will appreciate your talent.

Finally, if you enjoyed this book, please take the time to share your thoughts and post a review on Amazon. It'd be greatly appreciated!

Thank you and good luck!

Bonus Chapter: Selling Books on Amazon FBA

How to Go Lucrative Selling Physical Books Online

Do flashes of a sweaty workforce at your workshop, go-down or boutique cross your mind when you hear *physical products*? Well, sometimes it is inevitable, and that is one of the reasons many people avoid committing to selling physical products online. They think: I began to sell online so I do not have to buy distribution vans or deal with a long line of distributors, who are sometimes unreliable and occasionally sluggish. Would I really wish to go back to that same hassle?

Now, here is some good news. You can go on enjoying all the convenience of getting your product known online, even in the case of your books, and still sell your physical products via the net without cutting a sweat. In fact, you will not even need to have a personal distribution workforce. You will still sell your physical books and make an incredibly huge margin.

So then this is true about selling physical products?

- That it is not any harder to sell physical products than it is to sell otherwise?

- That it is not mandatory to have massive amounts of money in order to purchase inventory in order to start my business?

- That I shall not have to face hurdles of managing physical inventory?

- That I shall not have to deal with fussy customers?

- That the market for physical products is actually not saturated?

- That I can even make better business selling physical products online than I can while trying to earn affiliate income?

Sure – that is all true. There have been numerous misconceptions about selling physical products via the net, but once you understand that they all add up to the myth of not understanding the opportunities that exist, you will be ready to welcome your monthly thousands of dollars with a smile. In fact, for those who learnt the ropes sometime ago, earning up to $4000 per month, and $2000 when the month is not so great is not a big deal.

So, what are the real facts on selling physical products online?

For one, you do not have to do anything as the product owner, besides committing your item. How, exactly, does that take place? Well, simple: you just outsource the service at every stage – easy.

- You can get marketable inexpensive items to make up your inventory, thus confirming the fact that you do not have to have loads of cash to begin your online business.

- Very many people are looking to buy physical items online on a daily basis, and this confirms that the market is not saturated; and instead, it is growing bigger.

- You can get ways of starting your online business with minimal or no capital at all.

- That going affiliate is not as lucrative as selling physical products.

- That you can make everything very easy and convenient for you by letting Amazon to do the selling for you.

What we are going to pursue now is that last point on Amazon. Why go anywhere else when Amazon has the FBA package that offloads you of any physical and mental burden and you just watch your money flow in?

Incidentally, FBA aptly stands for *Fulfillment by Amazon*. Does a customer want your product delivered? Amazon does it. The customer needs something, let us say – swapped? Amazon still straightens that out nicely. You need to see the money because you are in business? You just look at your Amazon account. Is there excess inventory sitting around with Amazon? No problem – Amazon can divert it to eBay; after all what you want is the money. How more convenient can it get?

How FBA Works

How, for the love of a great profit, does this platform, FBA work? That must be something you are wondering, considering the market always seems competitive, and sometimes murky. Luckily, you are going to find all the necessary steps here, simply put and explicitly dealt with. Here are the main aspects that will reassure you about FBA:

1. Sending your inventory to an FBA center

Oh, oh... How do I do that? Well, no need to panic because that is very easy. You just get your shipment ready, of course, with the basic information including your address. Amazon will then consider the category of your product; its size; and such other minor but important details, and then determine the FBA center suited for your inventory. In fact, as soon as you complete the initial move, you will be able to see the destination address for your inventory.

That sounds easy – not much of a hassle and I know where my goods are...

But how safe is my inventory?

It is understandable that you should be concerned about the security of your products because you do not want your stuff lost, pilfered or delivered anywhere without guarantee for payment. That is why in these centers run by Amazon, you are assured of:

- Presence of security staff 24/7

- Storage of your products in very secure cages

Computerized order tracking that is automated; hence, it is free from manipulation.

Is there any special packaging required?

Well, Amazon would like your products to be well packaged to keep them safe from adverse elements. Just so you are sure that you are doing it right, and for convenience, you could purchase the packaging material right from Amazon. The material includes suitable poly bags; boxes; stretch wrap; bubble wrap; among other items.

Storage

Apart from the aspect of security that you have already been assured of, you need to know the following as well:

- That Amazon scans your products immediately on arrival and officially receives them at your designated FBA center.

- That Amazon takes the measurements for your products and records them accordingly, in order to get apt storage for them.

- That Amazon maintains a modern integrated system that allows you to monitor the movement of your inventory.

Your inventory at the FBA centers is conspicuous

Is that really possible? Well, that you might wonder because you are possibly imagining your products in a go-down. Well, with the FBAs, it would not really matter if your products were in a bunker or some other deeper zone. Amazon offers you ways of letting potential customers know that your products exist and that they are available for sale.

Is that not great! How does that happen?

Well, Amazon has offers for buyers as well, and that includes opportunities to acquire other products at a discount as they purchase their chosen products. So, in the process, your product stands a good chance of being seen by potential customers. This usually happens through:

i) The Buy Box

ii) Amazon Prime

iii) Free Super Saver Delivery

Do these platforms really work – you may wonder? And yes; they do work. In the UK, for example, sellers who use the FBA have reported an 85% sales increment. Others who do not care to go for special facilities but just join the FBA fraternity have had sales increments of 20% and upwards. You see with FBA, even customers who initially did not have your product in mind get to see it and get enticed to add it into their shopping cart. And so your sales keep rising without you incurring any extra cent.

Amazon is responsible for delivering your products

Really that happens? A customer makes an order and I do not have to do anything but wait for the payment? Well, it is one of those things that are as good as they sound. In fact, all across the countries in the European Union (EU) and the UK, you do not need to worry about making deliveries. The great Amazon sees to it that all products ordered from their FBA centers get to the customers in good time and in great shape.

Amazon saves you the problem of language barrier

When you are doing the selling personally, you are bound to have a language issue when you are English speaking and you want to sell to a Spanish speaking customer and so on. But Amazon is a global operator that deals with customers using their local languages. Do you see now that you will be able to reach a global populace more easily when selling via FBA centers than when you are selling through other avenues that are as limited as you are?

That is truly wonderful! You now want to begin selling your physical books through Amazon FBA.

This is how to begin the FBA business:

- Of course you have an account on Amazon; and if you do not, you are going to open one

- Now click *Inventory*.

- Then go to *Manage Inventory*

- Ask yourself: Which product do I want to sell through FBA? Once you have identified the product, click to tick against it within the column on the left

- Look at the drop down menu at *Actions*, and click against 'Change to Fulfilled by Amazon'.

- On the page that follows, do click *Convert*

The rest of the directions are straightforward and your product henceforth appears on the FBA listing.

Printed in Great Britain
by Amazon

58260071R00024